Knowing What's Enough

JOERG P. BIEBERNICK

Knowing What's Enough

A guide to a life of more fulfillment
and happiness within self-selected limits.

Bibliografische Information der Deutschen Nationalbibliothek.
Die Deutsche Nationalbibliothek verzeichnet diese Publikation in der
Deutschen Nationalbibliografie; detaillierte bibliografische Daten sind im
Internet über http://dnb.dnb.de abrufbar.

© 2023 Joerg Biebernick
Satz, Herstellung und Verlag:
BoD – Books on Demand, Norderstedt
ISBN 978-3-7568-2800-5

Content

Foreword 7

Introduction 11

Chapter 1 19
    Why it's up to everyone to determine what makes you happy 19

Chapter 2 27
    Happiness as the ultimate driver of individual motivation 27

Chapter 3 31
    1   Limitations and tradeoffs – Your Health 31
    2   Limitations and tradeoffs –Financial Resources 35

Chapter 4 41
    Drivers of your happiness – 41
    1   Physical Environment 41
    2   Professional Impact on Society 46
    3   Relationships 55
    4   Self Fulfillment 59
    5   Self reflection and Assessment 67
    6   Planning ahead 73
        1   Y1 Plan 73
        2   End State 77
        3   In-between milestones 80

About the author 83

Foreword

One does not have to be a genius to recognize that we as a human species are on an almost unstoppable path to self-destruction in terms of our impact on the planet. As I write these words, I can sense many of you object already, either believing that we will find a way through the crisis that's been building for the last 50+ years, or that the facts are exaggerated and that it won't be as bad as many predict. Looking at the facts though, CO_2 concentration in the earth's air has increased in a linear fashion without any interruption since at least 1960, despite the various pledges, commitments and summits.

I sincerely hope that I am wrong. It is simply that I see a few truths getting in the way of the collective finding a sustained way out of this potentially devastating path for planet earth.

First, it is unlikely that most country states will self-limit over time the number of resources used for GDP growth in the broader sense. After all, democratically elected governments are under performance accountability towards their constituents. As such, they must deliver on the agenda that matters most to their citizens. As this agenda is driven, by and large, first by economic growth, wealth, employment and in the broader sense by "more is better", governments will find it hard to self-restrict in the form of regulations that reduce growth and prosperity as a sacrifice for the planet. After all, there will always be a democratic contender who is willing to promise a richer future and hence, readily replace any such incumbent that is associated with less wealth creation.

Needless to say that an autocratic head of state would likely care even less for the planet, as he is least accountable to anyone but himself.

Secondly, countries are in competition with each other. Even if there was a consensus in one country of size to keep a government in place that would want to balance growth with sustainability, chances are that there would remain many countries who would opt out of such self-restrain for a myriad of reasons, to gain "advantage" if nothing else. It is tough to imagine places where the majority of its citizens live close to the poverty line, to step back and join those wealthy nations in their regulatory restraint. I have heard the argument already, in that those wealthy nations have brought planet earth to where it is now by getting rich, and now it would be not up to the poorer, less developed countries to come to the rescue. Fair point from their POV. If you think I exaggerate, just look at how tough it is to get to a minimum tax rate for corporations around the world. Countries are tempted to provide lower rates and to hence attract investment. I am afraid the same logic will also apply to environmental regulations.

Thirdly, companies are in competition with each other on a mostly global scale, enabled by trade agreements and global supply chains. They have no choice but to produce where it is most cost advantageous to serve their markets, as they compete with a price-setter in every category, dictated by the lowest cost producer less their ability to differentiate in a meaningful way. In other terms, if one country is overly regulating them with cost impacts, they will move elsewhere to compete better.

For all three reasons, I don't see regulation from countries to be the savior of our climate crisis. It will not be the supply side that will save us. Sustained change has to be rooted in the demand side of things. It is the citizens of countries and the world as such that have to change the way they look at success and happiness. As long as happiness equals more, bigger, faster, higher without any limit, we will be unlikely to change our current trajectory. Unfortunately, the wealthiest citizens of planet Earth are not exactly a role model for contentment. Instead, it seems like the ultimate quest of wealth is to burn fossil fuels for space tourism.

Only when we all individually come to realize first what is enough for our own personal happiness can there be lasting change. Only when we are happy to say "no" to more, bigger and newer more frequently, will our resource impact on the planet slow down in a sustained fashion. To be clear, I am a keen believer in democracy and free market capitalism per se. I am far from pushing a socialistic, supply constraining agenda and don't want to be misunderstood. My believe is in insight and education to achieve a sustained change in consumer behavior, leading to a sustained improvement of life on the planet.

It is long evident that happiness in nations is not increasing at the same pace as GDP/ capita. Happiness in the US, for instance, has not significantly increased since the 70s. If anything, it has unfortunately decreased, and that despite wealth increasing. Similarly, studies have shown that happiness on an individual level only correlates with income up until a sum of 80,000 USD per year is achieved – give or take a few dollars. Despite these facts, people seemingly still believe that wealthier means happier.

This book is a humble contribution to hopefully helping a few people to realize the power of enough. Instead of looking at money as a maximization function, the book considers money as a mere limiter to what one can do at any given point in time. Like health, it is hence not a goal in and of itself, but a constraint. Happiness will come from other drivers intrinsically linked to human nature.

Who knows, maybe the book will lead to a few tons less CO_2 being produced. By now, it's all about marginal gains going forward!

Enjoy the book and good luck in achieving a happy, fulfilled life knowing yourself and what is enough for you.

Introduction

I vividly remember the winter of 1994 when I lived as a recently hired employee of a leading consumer goods company in Frankfurt, Germany.

It had been 2 years since I joined probably the most prestigious company in the area of my interest, after I graduated from one of the best business schools in Germany. By all measures I had already a lot to be proud of for my young age and was set for what could potentially become a very rewarding career.

I had recently moved into a bigger apartment in a nice area of Frankfurt, surrounded by bars, gyms and other infrastructure that should make for a convenient living.

It was hence rather strange that for the second time during these two initial years of my time in this company, I had a hard time maintaining my motivation. Almost every day I felt that it was tough to get out of bed in the morning, to get dressed and make the trip to the offices outside of town. I could not really point to any issue, item, person or other event though, making it tough to problem-solve for what was increasingly feeling like my first mid-life crisis. The biggest worry was that I was just about to start my life, I felt like I was supposed to take off. Instead, I felt increasingly like something had to change, or else I would become a failure.

The next thing I remember was getting stuck in the usual evening traffic coming back from work. I recall that I was annoyed about the big city inconveniences like traffic jams, eating into the precious time I could otherwise use to do things that are more pleasurable. I recall seeing a grey-haired driver of a luxury BMW sedan to my right. He looked similarly bored or borderline annoyed as I did. It struck me that the only thing potentially separating him from me were 30 years of work, a few thousand dollars more on the bank account et al. Still, he was feeling the same, independent of his wealth and stature because he was living the same reality as I was. I think it was back then that it dawned on me for the first time that money alone was not linked to a massive change in happiness. Other factors had to come to play.

It would be nice if I could claim that a change of my lifestyle and to my lack of motivation followed this incident. Unfortunately, that was not yet the case. It was rather another morning, not sure anymore when exactly that winter, when I realized that the last time I had signs of a crisis was also in November, pretty much exactly a year earlier. It was then that a big light bulb seemingly went on and a realized that what I thought to be a job-related issue, was more likely pure and simple weather related.

What I had found was that a) weather patterns were an important part of my happiness drivers and b) that I was not very good in linking my emotional state to a particular driver. I was rather lost in the connection between how I felt, and what most likely caused the feeling.

That again was scary, as I imagined the consequences of falsely believing that the cure to my crisis was a change in job environment, only to end up as unhappy in the next company.

It was exactly then that I decided to bring some order into my unknown drivers of satisfaction and happiness.

For the next 3 months I wrote down on little post-it notes everytime and everything that either gave me a spout of bliss, of happiness, joy or of the opposite: of frustration, anger, irritation. The situations included much of the mundane, from a hard bed mattress to traffic jams, noise from the street below at night, the grey weather in November on the negative side. I deliberately did not try to systemize too early, but to prevent my mind from structuring the experiences.

The same obviously applied to the positive moments. Moments of sharing a drink with a good friend after work, the feeling of bliss after my run in the nearby park, the blue sky after many days of grey, etc.

You get the picture, I am sure. In hindsight, I did something that is extremely powerful. I did not search for the drivers of my happiness in concepts like financial wealth or superior achievements like a promotion, a lifelong career. I was lucky to look for instants of happiness. The underlying belief I had was that if I shifted the balance of moments of unhappiness towards more moments of happiness, in sum my life would feel better.

So, after 3 months of diligent notetaking, I sat down to face the mountain of post-its on my desk. First, I simply grouped the notes into the plusses and the minuses. That helped me realize that many sources of happiness for me had a direct opposite that was equally controllable and likely to occur. The example of being stuck in a traffic jam, for instance, had its positive in an approximately "30 min morning and evening commute, allowing me to unwind". Interestingly, I was now knowing that some commuting time was making me happy, just not in excess of 30 minutes, all the time.

Stepping back a bit more, I realized certain dimensions behind my post-it piles.

For starters, a lot of notes were dealing with my "physical environment". My room, my apartment, its location and distance to parks, the office, restaurants, gyms etc., the town I lived in, the absence of bodies of water like lakes or the ocean, but its positive proximity to forests to recharge on the weekend, the weather in the fall, winter and spring which did not make us for the few nice weeks in the summer... All these played a role, it seemed. Whilst many of them were not immediately changeable, it dawned on me that over time, I could introduce choice and change. I also noticed that not all of the changes would be free of charge. An apartment on a less noisy street may cost more, asking me to trade off some spending power vs. a better gym for instance.

Another big pile of post-its had to do with my professional role. None of my post-its had anything to do with a salary increase or a promotion, for the simple reason that I had not received one in the 3 months of my "research". Still, there were plenty of moments related to making connections, achieving something of value to others, winning together vs. competitors and so forth. What I had stumbled on without realizing it much was the dimension of "having an impact on others, on society". Literature is filled with evidence that we as human beings draw meaning from actively helping others. We may call it work or in some cases nonpaid work, donations, charity work etc. The core is though the same – we work and help others not only to make ends meet. We do it because we need to gain satisfaction from our impact on those around us. It's innate in our nature. I had just stumbled on it with my specific elements of where I felt I can be best in having an impact.

Thirdly, and very distinctly, I had several post-its related to the connections I had and those newly made. Again, thirty years and many books later, it is less of a surprise that we all feed on the connections we have with family, friends, far or close. You may ask – so what is the big insight here?

Well, let me fast forward 20 years to a time when I was permanently updating my Facebook account with where I had been, what I had done or seen, eaten, with whom and shared all this with many "connections", called friends by the app. I realized that those posts and seeing others' posts was actually not making me happy. It was no comparison to the meaningful interactions I had at parties, in bars or friends' homes. I felt annoyed by the portrayal of idealized people posing at exceptional places and in moments that I could not share with them. It pushed me more away from friends rather than bringing me closer. Therefore, I stopped using Facebook and never even started with Instagram or Twitter. So not so trivial after all – real connections with others are a key driver worth facing up to, and becoming clear who it is that makes us happy, how and when in which form of interaction, more so now than ever, I'd argue.

Let's come back to the remaining dimensions behind my piles of sticky notes.

I also had a few notes that related to activities and experiences that did not have really anything to do with much else other than practicing activities that gave me a deep sense of self fulfillment. Those were activities and moments not linked to others necessarily or done with an impact on others in mind. They related most always to physical or spiritual experiences such as spending a night out at the opera, listening to an amazing voice that captured the beauty of an emotion in an instant, just to disappear after the curtain had fallen. Or the moment linked to riding my motorcycle at night under a star lit sky at relatively quick speed (yes). I called this dimension, self-fulfillment.

One more observation I would like to share upfront, as it's critical for the rest of what you may choose to read: at no point did the pursuit of wealth, or the desire to live 100 years make it to my list of moments captured. You may now say what is so surprising about that, as these are concepts and are hence unlikely to trigger instant emotions. They are linked to hope, an idea about a better future, about happiness postponed or experienced in some distant moment later.

Fair enough, but isn't it a bit strange that most of society functions based on the idea that more wealth equals more happiness, and that more and longer health equals more and longer moments of joy? We will discuss this later in more depth.

For now, the exercise I did back then, almost 30 years ago, taught me a lot about what my personal subtractors and multipliers of personal happiness were. I turned those drivers subsequently into a rough plan on what I would like to do professionally by when and where and how I would like to live. Most importantly, I was deeply aware of the various relationships in my life and their impact on my emotional state, including the pleasure of getting to know new people and learning from them. In one word, I was much more aware of myself and my emotional fabric.

All this allowed me to then determine the likely financial requirements to afford those elements that are linked to material expense. Without remembering the specific details on how much I would have needed as capital and income over the duration of the plan back then, I did realize that after all, the numbers were not at all outrageous given my likely career trajectory. That felt quite reassuring, taking one source of potential anxiety away very early in my life.

From conversations with most of my friends still today, it is precisely this worry about the ability to afford one's future lifestyle that causes a lot of angst. I hope that this book will help many to understand what is really needed to enable a happy, content and fulfilled life, without drowning in worries about finances or old age.

Chapter 1

Why it's up to everyone to determine what makes you happy

In theory, I cannot imagine many people will disagree with the need to understand what makes us happy on an individual basis, and then to draw a line and declare this as being enough. Not necessarily as a precise science, but as a broad stroke concept. Still, it's fascinating to observe that virtually no one from our private or public life seems to practice this obvious choice.

Part of it can certainly be explained by a general inability to identify the drivers of happiness and degrees required on each driver to be happy. This book will aim to address this problem, helping hopefully many people to get in touch with their inner self, to better understand who they are and what they require to be more content in all important aspects of their lives.

Just as an example, let's imagine someone finds out that a key driver for inner peace and contentment is "to frequently enjoy a great view over nature". Now, such view can come in the form of a large mansion overlooking an expensive strip of coast in the Mediterranean, or in a small house or even apartment overlooking the coast. The difference in financial requirements between the two can easily be a factor of 10x. Now, if one has the means to afford the more costly option AND be able to fulfill all other relevant and important needs to be happy, then there is no issue to committing all funds required to this lovely mansion.

However, it is more likely that the mansion is a far distant dream in terms of affordability. In this case, the negative consequences are first a certain sense of dissatisfaction, an inability to afford what is (falsely) assumed as a key enabler to a higher state of happiness.

Second, it may lead to years of activities destined to enable the purchase of such estate, spending time not necessarily doing things that are ideally suited to fulfill one's needs to contribute to society in a meaningful way, but in a way that maximizes income per se. You probably can identify with this right now, or you know several close friends who have jobs in careers that are not necessarily making them happy but are delivering the maximum return for their invested time. Surely, that cannot be very fulfilling in the here and now – there is just hope that once all the hard-earned cash is used to buy the luxury mansion, an overwhelming feeling of happiness will compensate for the years of suffering.

Ultimately, one has to decide for oneself if this equation works. I argue, though, that the alternative of reaching the driver of happiness (a nice view over nature) sooner in an affordable form (the fictious apartment for a tenth of the price) will a) deliver many moments of happiness for years and b) offer optionality in terms of how to spend the working hours in the most satisfying ways without the pressure at the end of each month to make ends meet, aiming for that mighty prize in the distant future.

Let's look at happiness though through the macro lens of society. I would argue that it is common knowledge that ever increasing standards of living measured in financial terms as per capita income are NOT driving or even correlating with increased levels of happiness in society. The subject of the connection between wealth and happiness in society has been researched all over, is tracked in many countries, and does shockingly not increase in many of the rich nations of this planet for several years. In fact, in several countries, national happiness is going backwards, despite regular increases of per capita income. Interestingly, very often the assumed explanations can be found in the lack of quality in the drivers that this book will discuss.

For example, the recent decrease in happiness in the USA is attributed (also) to the increase in digital media, and specifically social networks such as Facebook, Twitter et al. The hypothesis is that as people spend more time in virtual connections, they have less time for offline, "real" connections. Whether or not this is true for society is probably the subject to extensive fact-finding research. I will argue though that on an individual basis, one can find out very efficiently if digital connections can make one happy or not, using the contents of this book. I realized very much that sharing great moments online with so-called friends made me feel more unhappy, jealous and pressured. The natural consequence was to wean myself off what made me unhappy, and to spend more time in real-life relations.

Let us do an experiment: Who would agree that ultimate happiness can only be found if one owns a 500 feet super yacht, 2 private jets, one house in NYC, one in the Hamptons, one on the French riviera and one estate in Africa – plus the odd 10+ car collection? Importantly, you need to own ALL of these trophy possessions before you can feel a sense of accomplishment and happiness.

Crazy, no? I assume hardly any of us would agree that these are the sort of items required in totality before happiness can be found. Why for instance would one need 2 private jets? Would one not be enough? Why does it have to be a 500+ feet sized yacht, why would 400, 200 or yet even 100 feet not be enough? Why would one need to own any of the quoted mansions and estates when one can potentially rent any of them, or a smaller version of them.

Exactly right. But why is it then that those people that own a part of my fictious scenario, and smaller scaled versions of it, are in the large majority still striving for more? Why do they not stop at one estate, one or two cars? Why do they compare themselves permanently with others that have a partially bigger set of trophies they call their own? The latter is the big question we need to address, as it is not allowing society and its individuals to obtain mass contentment, and it's not sustainable for the planet either.

Very clearly, our planet is choking under the stress we put it under. Our energy and resource consumption are such that it will make life as we like it difficult to sustain. The effects are noticeable everywhere, and more and more often.

The tricky bit is that we live in a world where those who consume most resources are the minority, impacting the lives of current and future generations of everyone else living on this planet. Those "have nots" on the global scale, living in underdeveloped countries in Africa, Asia and the Middle East are likely having the same dreams as those already living the life of wealth and abundance. Its unfathomable to imagine everyone in Asia consuming at the same level as the average US American for instance. The world will not be able to sustain such consumption and the related emissions.

One may argue that it can only be the natural right of anyone living on this planet, to aim for such wealth accumulation as in the developed world. It is portrayed as a role model in countless movies and TV series. After all, one of the first items that can be found in virtually any house in a developing country is a TV screen – projecting the aspirational world of Hollywood and Bollywood to billions of households. Who could credibly stand up against what is universally showcased as a successful, desirable lifestyle?

One can hardly see any democratically elected government being very popular for long if they wanted to keep its population resource constrained for the greater good of life on this planet. Someone else would come along, run for office and promise a more attractive alternative and surely get the popular vote. This can hence not be the answer in a democracy. The answer can only lie within each individual, realizing that happiness is not linked to an ever-increasing quantity of possessions. To be clear, I would be the last person to argue that several aspects of existence and happiness require financial means. This is also largely confirmed by research, stating that as of a certain income level (around 80,000 USD per annum), happiness of a person is no longer correlated with increasing financial means. However up until such level, it very much does, as is understandable.

In summary, the concept of finding sustained happiness through knowing what the underlying drivers are, and deducting what material needs are hence related, is of essence for all of us to find more happiness while we live, without over proportionally taking a toll on our already stretched planet.

There is yet another critical underlying reason why finding happiness now with enough or reduced means is essential.

Unfortunately, there is a second limitation to our ability to enjoy life. We will spend some more time discussing it further down in the book. Upfront though, it's very clear that our current state of health has a direct impact on our ability to enjoy life today, and on our likelihood to be able to enjoy future years of wellness.

If I am overweight today, chances are my joints will suffer over proportionately. This may not only lead to several weight related issues such as heart problems, diabetes etc., but prematurely limit our ability to move. Hence, several activities that would make us happy, such as travel, walking with friends, sports of all sorts, playing with grandchildren, may be significantly reduced.

So, whilst our financial means may indeed rise over the years, and hence allow the example of a major house purchase with a wonderful view to be possible, one cannot lose line of sight that at the same time, our health potential is on an irreversible downward trend, ending with death.

The opportunity lies in the sweet spot of enough means to enjoy what makes life special whilst our body can support us.

By now I think everyone having read these lines is keenly aware of the opportunity that is implicit in the Knowing What's Enough.

You may now want to argue that it is naïve to assume that the adoption of the content of this book (and others I am sure) will be enough to make the world happier, and to prevent an environmental melt down.

To those I would say that it is all about marginal gains and challenge what could be the alternative. Marginal gains seem little when only one individual produces them, but here again power lies in mass adoption.

After all, if every person having read this book does what is on average the case, to tell approx. 10 people about the positive difference the content made to their lives, then you can see a path to a significant impact on many individuals and society as a hole. Why not even imagine a teaching module in a related class as mandatory in every child's upbringing? My children certainly had classes around the theory of knowledge, philosophy or even religion. The inclusion of the concept of Knowing What is Enough would rank high on any scale of teaching in my most humble pov.

Chapter 2

Happiness as the ultimate driver of individual motivation

"Assumptions are what kill you" I recall a former boss telling me. Rightly so, if you assume something and base your decisions and actions on it, just to be shown later that your assumption was flawed, you will find that you wasted resources, including time without achieving what you aimed for. Testing assumptions is hence a valid exercise before one embarks on a long endeavor.

My critical assumption for this book, and for my life, is that we are all ultimately driven by the desire to achieve what one can simply call happiness. Let us dissect this a bit more.

First, by happiness I don't speak of the fleeting feeling of happiness related to laughing after a good joke. It is rather the kind of emotion that we would call contentment, life satisfaction, well-being and even joy.

Someone once told me that the difference between a great and an average life is the number of moments that leave you breathless. Or put differently, it is not the number of heart beats you count in your life, but the number of moments that made your heart stop in awe.

Don't take these ideas quite literally please. What I am trying to put in words though is that happiness is not some ambitious goal out there in the future, linked to any kind of achievement of status, wealth, looks, reputation or power. Those are ideas about what may make us happier, without any proof that they will. It would be very disappointing to achieve whatever IT may be, just to realize that its effect was fleeting if at all there.

The kind of happiness I am talking about is proven to be present in your life, because of how you were able to identify the activity, moment, situation that either made you very happy, or which distracted from your contentment to such degree that you took note. It is not a theoretical concept, and its deeply personal. No one else may find all the same happiness drivers in another person. I figure they are as individualistic as our fingerprints.

Now that we are clearer about what I mean when we discuss happiness as a desirable state in this book, lets deal with another challenge I heard every now and then.

Some people argue that happiness, even when defined as we did, is not the goal in anyone's life. Alternative life goals I was told were for instance:

- To serve your country
- To be a law-abiding citizen
- To be a good Christian / Muslim et al
- To be a role model of a father, husband, son, leader, CEO

All these goals are seemingly sensible and honorable to pursue. There are only two issues with them in my pov.

First, they depend more or less on the perspective of someone else to be validated. How will you know that you have been a role model of a father, CEO etc. other than by the perception and feedback of others. You will hence put your life's worth, your sense of dignity and satisfaction, into the perceived degree to which you were serving your country, respected the law or behaved like the best father there is. From all I know, one of the biggest fatalities there can be is to put your emotional state in a dependency of someone else, an external driver that one has very little control over.

Secondly, and you saw this already from my past tense used above, whether you have been the best you can be in the eyes of others is usually a judgement at the END of a certain period. Would you want to live your entire life trying to achieve your life goal, without any or many periods of joy and happiness, just to potentially ultimately get the final badge of accomplishment (or not).

You think this is pure fiction? Maybe not. Movies have been made of lifetime stories of public servants believing they were serving a just cause, to find out later in their lives that not everything was so just after all, to then go on a rampage or at least be deeply depressed. Great movie material isn't it, as long as it is not your life being told.

To be clear, I don't argue that living along certain principles like the above mentioned can be part of anyone's personal code to achieve happiness. What I am challenging is that behind it all, other than achieving life satisfaction through happiness, there are not many other valid motivations.

If you, however, fundamentally disagree with the assumption that achieving moments or periods of sustained happiness during your life are not the ultimate, worthwhile driver for most everything in your life, then please feel free to stop reading further, because most of the rest of the book is based on this fundamental assumption.

Besides, most of the above mentioned, worthwhile pursuits in life such as serving your country, being a good father etc., ultimately make you happy – that's why you enjoy many aspects of being a father. Sure, you do them because that's just what is expected of you in this moment, but lets be honest, there is a lot of contentment in raising children for instance.

Similarly, most altruistic activities are not so altruistic. There is a deep sense of contentment linked to doing good to others, giving is making us happy as a species. That's nothing to be ashamed of, if we do good by being selfish. It is important though to listen to our inner emotional voice and become aware of it, so we can decide to consciously do more of it.

In other words, the above-mentioned life goals are most likely linked to activities that make you feel good in the moment, satisfied, content. If that's the case, chances are you will enjoy the rest of the book, and chances are also that your mentioned life goal is at least one element worth pursuing, as its part of your personal fabric of happiness.

Now that we talked about quite a bit the assumption of happiness as a key driver for our life, it is time to introduce the framework we will use going forward to get the most life satisfaction possible here and now, whilst respecting the tradeoffs to happiness tomorrow and further in the future.

Chapter 3

1   Limitations and tradeoffs – Your Health

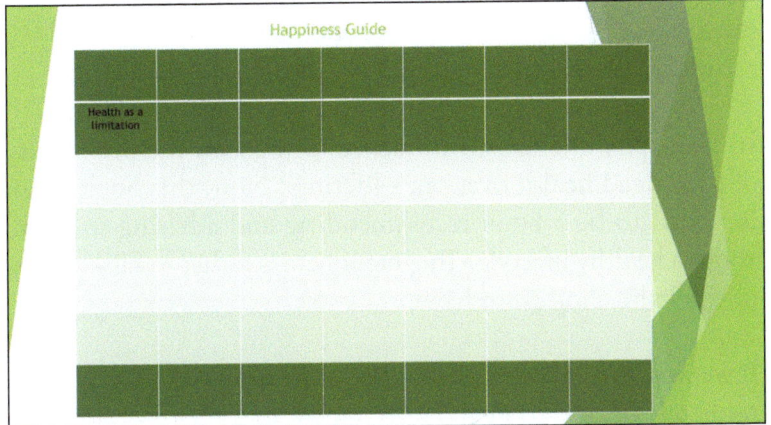

Let me introduce the first limitation to happiness, satisfaction and a sense of accomplishment now in a more deliberate way: your health.

To most of us it is intuitively clear that our state of physical health is a natural enabler for our existence. If by existing, we mean not only our ability to reason, but to move without pain or restriction and to fully use our five senses, then the health of our body is a critical to happiness. Without a fully functioning body, we may still experience moments of joy and pleasure, lead a fruitful life and leave a legacy behind, but within increased limits vs. an alternative body with close to perfect health.

We must acknowledge that happiness can also be found in moments and activities that require very few bodily functions to still be operational. Anyone doubting this only needs to spend some time with people who lost limbs, the sense of sight or hearing through sickness or accidents. Within their new limits, most people find new meaning and a sense of happiness – a terrific adjustment of the mind and heart.

In principle, one has an influence to increase the probability of prolonged health over one's lifetime. Now, this book is not intended to be a book recommending and advising in detail about a healthy lifestyle. The intent here is rather to raise awareness for the choices we have.

If we were to aim to only maximize our happiness today, without trade off consideration about tomorrow and the days after, one could imagine a rather hedonistic lifestyle of indulgence in the pleasures of food, drink etc. The marginal contribution to our happiness would decrease by overdoing those activities that if enjoyed scarcely, would have brought a certain pleasure. They will also likely take a toll on our health and hence ability to enjoy many decades of unrestricted happiness.

As to the diminishing return of happiness of certain activities or situations when they are to be repeated too often, there have been books written about this as well. For example, the first cappuccino after having spent weeks in places that only offer simple filter coffee, tastes delicious. The 5th cappuccino of the day does not have the same effect.

I recall discovering golf as a challenging sport at the age of 25. Being enthusiastic as I was, I decided to go on a golf vacation in Tunisia. After 3 days of playing 18-27 holes a day, I could not be bothered to go out a 4th day to repeat the activity. My hands, feet and back were hurting, and more so, the pleasure I got from the rare indulgence of golf was replaced by an almost work like monotony.

Going back to health, you must come to the realization that some investment into your health today may bear fruit in increased happiness tomorrow.

I don't suggest making a science out of this aspect of the framework. For example, health is not a replacement for self-fulfillment. Let's talk about that. One's desire, for instance, to run a marathon, or to climb a mountain of a certain height, has nothing to do with the health limitation we are talking about. Achieving those goals fit the category of the happiness driver I call "Self-Fulfillment" and we will discuss it later. These elements are critical for a balanced sense of happiness, besides the other, equally important ones. Health however comes only to play as a limitation to achieving those goals.

Put differently, if you learn that running races gives you a big sense of accomplishment and fulfillment, then you probably will need to have a different health plan than someone for whom just remaining in "age adjusted health" is sufficient for his happiness driving activities.

Health is a result, a limitation and enabler to the other drivers, not a goal in and of itself.

Let me try and illustrate my own case over the years. More than 20 years ago I felt a lot of joy trekking and climbing mountains. I hence had a "self-fulfillment" plan to climb the highest trekkable mountain in Nepal, the highest mountain in Africa and in Europe. I gave myself a loose time frame of 5+ years, because there was no rush needed, and I'd be looking forward to each event even more if it was spaced out a bit.

To be sure I would accomplish these goals, my health plan changed 12 months before each trip from something along the following, base health plan:

- 30 min run, 3-4 times per week
- Weekend hikes in mountains
- 1 times per week strength training
- 7.5 h of sleep

To something more along the following lines, aiming to build stamina for the strenuous hikes ahead:

- 45-60 min run 4x min per week
- 2x strength training, focusing on legs and back

No major shift on a piece of paper, but a big shift in the kind of fitness I was able to obtain. Naturally, once I had done Mont Blanc, Mera Peak (failed on last day and had to be flown out after typhoon) and Kilimanjaro, I went back to my sustaining health plan, pretty much in place up until this very day. As a result, my weight has remained unchanged over the last 22 years – quite an accomplishment one could say.

So let us park the content of what will go into this dimension of our action plan for now, and have a look at the other major limitation, financial resources.

2   Limitations and tradeoffs –Financial Resources

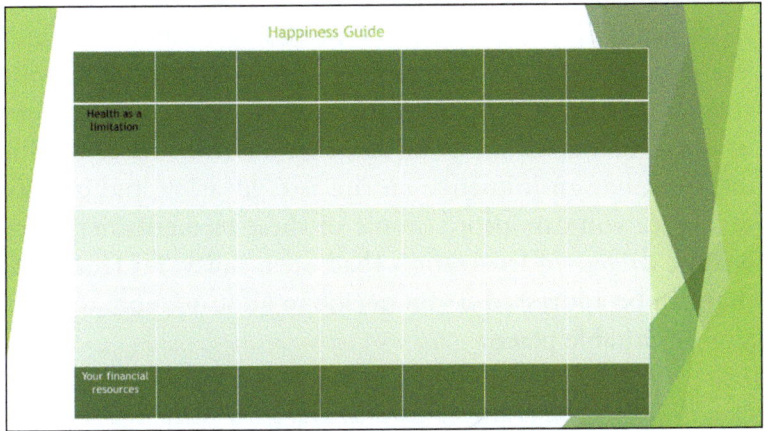

As mentioned earlier in this book, the number of financial resources available in terms of income and equity today, will have an influence on those elements of your happiness drivers that require money.

First, let me be clear, many elements of your happiness will be largely or to some degree disconnected from your financial means. Especially the area we will discuss in terms of relationships and connections, but also self-fulfillment and to some degree your physical environment, don't necessarily require large financial resources. We will discuss this in a bit in this book.

Still, some of your activities and your physical environment will forcibly be influenced by either your income and or your available equity.

Income is, as we know, what you take home each week or month after you accounted for taxes and social security or other deductions. You have a choice on what to do with it. Some of it you will need to spend on life's necessities like food, heating, gas, insurance, rent etc. Not all of it though is a true fix cost. This book will put some light into your choices on how much you want to allocate to each element in order to maximize your satisfaction from it. Rent, for instance, has an influence on the size, location and quality of a place you can afford. Some of these elements may very well be drivers of frustration (bad area, noisy, far from job) that can be addressed if you decide to allocate more to it for a more suitable place.

Assuming your income is for now stable, it is then a question of tradeoffs with other elements of your spend. For instance, you can decide to spend less on your car going forward, as you may find out through the exercise in this book that a big car is not a significant driver of your happiness, or maybe even a frustrater (tough to find parking). In that case you will have an easy choice to be made when you can, meaning when your rental contract and your car lease come up for renewal.

It may, however, not always be that easy to find a spend bucket that you can (and want) to easily reduce in order to enable investments into another.

In that case, equity comes into play. Equity is essentially cash that you have not yet spent but have invested it to gain a certain return to enable more future spend. Again, this book does not want to argue for or against saving and certainly will not prescribe a certain amount or percentage of any reader's income.

Rather, I want to highlight the concept of time-0deferred consumption, to enable a future choice that you believe will positively influence your happiness in a sustained way.

Let me give one personal example. At some point in my life, I was clear that I wanted to have a family, likely 2 children. To be comfortable, this would require a bigger house to live in. Ideally, a place with 4 bedrooms, allowing myself and my wife, each of the children and the odd invited guest to have their own, private space. By looking around and doing some research, I found out what a house of this spec would cost to acquire in the area that was consistent with my other physical happiness drivers (e.g. view, close to town, green spaces close by, calm). Clearly this kind of place was significantly more expensive than the 2 bedroom apartment we then rented in town. I hence figured out how much I would need as down payment for an acceptable monthly mortgage payment and that amount went as a target into financial requirement plan, translated into an annual and monthly savings objective.

It sounds more complicated than it really is, and I assume that many of you practice this already intuitively. Putting it on a piece of paper makes it more powerful. What you will aim for is no longer an arbitrary (e.g. "1 million and I am happy") number. It will be the sum of the items that are closely tied to your proven happiness drivers. It is rooted in what makes you happy and it will be enough.

Critically, your required financial resources are a RESULT of your happiness plan, they are not a disjoint, unrelated maximization function. No longer will you feel like a slave to the so-called rat race, where everyone constantly only aims to chase "more" for the sake of "more".

You will feel differently, because you know what ENOUGH is for you, and only for you. This may not be the number that anyone else requires. It will take you out of the comparative nature of chasing financial returns.

For example, many of my friends ask themselves what the number is that they will require to be able to retire in peace and happiness. First, by following the guidance of this book to the end, this will not be an abstract question for you. You will be able to come up with a number that is pretty much rooted in what is likely going to be enough to make you happy as you retire. It is likely not the same lifestyle that you have to afford whilst you are in a young family, with school or university aged children...

Second, you may be surprised how small the number will be, taking everything into consideration. And as said before, knowing the number early on in your life will give you the very best chance of hitting or even exceeding it, without much effort. Sounds too optimistic?

Let's do one example here. Assume you are 30 years old today, have saved 20,000 and would like to retire at the age of 65. Your life expectancy is say 85, meaning you have to cover 20 years of expenses. Your expenses are likely reduced in retirement by 25%, given that your children are independent, and your activity reduces somewhat over time. By saving 20,000 per year, over 35 years, you will be able to retire with close to 3 MM in investments! That in return will enable you to spend almost 23,000 per month in retirement, which after inflation is equivalent to approx. 10,000 net after tax income today. No bad for the discipline to save 1,666 per month. The power is in

a) starting earlier and having time on your side,
b) the discipline of not wavering your savings plan for an instant gratification and,
c) the effects of compound interest rate.

To be clear, I assumed the average 7% return an investment into a non-managed, global ETF that you can buy as of 100 USD per share. Inflation is assumed to be at a long-term average of 2.5%, which is what most central banks aim for. All very reasonable assumptions.

Lastly, your number will not have to be compared with any of your friends. Remember, by quoting bigger, more audacious financial requirements those friends are most likely putting themselves under quite some emotional pressure for a long period of their lifetime. One can only hope that the suffering is worth it and rooted in what will make them happy!

I am deliberately spending quite some time on the concept of financial resources as a limitation, as I assume that for most of us, this is a true paradigm shift. You may not fully see this yet, because we have not gone through the exercise that will show you what you really need to be happy. Chances are, to stay with my prior outrageous example, it's not a private jet or 2, and not that big super yacht that you will need in your physical environment to be happy. That's all that matters.

Chapter 4

Drivers of your happiness –

1 Physical Environment

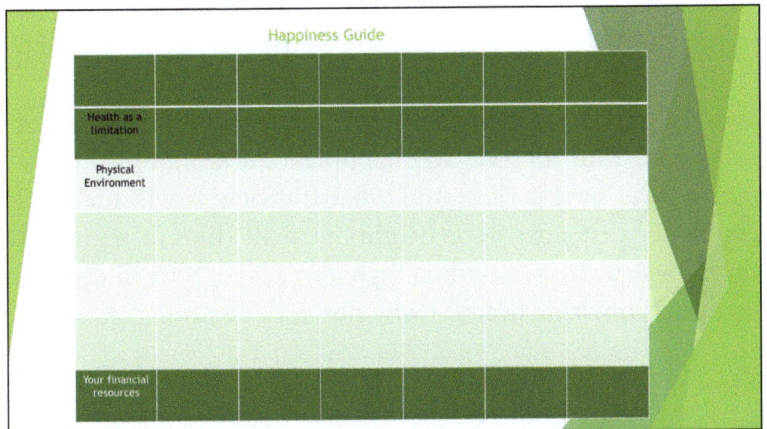

The critical assumption that this book uses is that everything that surrounds us has a potential impact to make us either more content, or less so. I would argue its not a risky assumption in the grand scheme of things. Entire industries depend on the assumption. Think home improvement, home decoration, the travel industry for example. We strive to be comfortable in our home. We strive to live in a part of town, or outside of town for that matter, that corresponds to our life needs. We aim to live in a certain distance to work, to the airport, to schools, to major shopping centers, to anything our life requires on a frequent basis.

I leave it up to the reader to decide how far you want to go in dissecting your physical environment into slices that may influence your happiness. For starters, let me give a few basic dimensions for starters and discuss them briefly:

Your place

By this I am referring to the apartment, condo or house you live in most of the time. Your primary residence one could call it.

Clearly, how and where this place is located will have a huge impact on your lifestyle and happiness. Its size probably matters. It may have a view, and what the view is will matter. It could be your next door neighbor's wall (like in many city dwellings), a street, a park, a highway, a lake, river or even the open ocean with a beach – why not, let's dream!

Most likely you will find out that noise, traffic, access to restaurants, bars, shops, schools, airports, work and others play a critical role. I, for instance, learned that I liked a 30 min trip to and from work to prepare mentally and to unwind. Anything much longer would annoy me or anything shorter would leave me feel not ready to face what's next in my day. Back then, this was a bit of a surprise to me.

Another layer more of granularity is to look inside your place. How comfortable is your furniture, the sofa, the bed, the desk chair you may work from? Is the light bothering you? Is it too hot, too cold?

You get a picture of how granular your satisfaction drivers can go. Don't feel bad about it being so executional. Happiness is not linked to some theoretical concept, but to many, seemingly benign, daily moments that can either frustrate or delight you.

I, for once, am delighted every time I sit down in my new office chair that has lumbar support. It's a detail, I know, but what a difference it makes when I write this book with delight vs. annoyance.

Your city

I grew up in a 4000-soul village, am living now in a 2000 people village with 500 cows, and have lived in several multi-million people metropolis. All these places had a profound impact on my life, either enabling certain activities and giving access to infrastructure, or limiting the same.

Several aspects of big cities may make you extremely happy. For example, they give access to an amazing choice of restaurants, theaters, music halls, night clubs, libraries, museums et al. They also bring many bright, educated people together, creating many challenging, interesting jobs. They usually come with a convenient travel infrastructure to whizz you around the country or the world.

On the other side, they produce smog, come along with sometimes excruciating traffic problems, noise and light pollution, high costs for scarce goods, such as spacious living quarters.

They may or may not offer sufficient access to green spaces to renew your soul, to let you walk, run and play in a park, by a river, lake or beach.

All these elements of a city can highly influence the lifestyle you can lead, its cost, and convenience.

I, for instance, am extremely happy where we now settled, outside Geneva, Switzerland, close to the lake and only 20 min away from the airport. Everything I can wish for is pretty much readily available, most of the year. Many of my closest friends are not surprisingly ex expats turned locals who equally fell in love with this place and will now never want to leave.

But every now and then, I do encounter the rare person who does not fall in love with what so perfectly fits my drivers of happiness. Not surprisingly, their needs are badly met here: There is generally not much of a night life to speak of (in comparison, with say, London). Similarly, the number of art exhibitions and museums is adequate for a city of 400,000 people, but not up to the standards of New York, London or Paris – how could they? Also, people speak mostly French here. Now, if you don't happen to speak French, it can be quite tedious to learn it, or be confronted with people who just don't want to understand you in English.

I mention the above just to showcase how one's happy place can be another person's boredom...

Your country

Now it gets a bit tricky. Everyone is forcibly born in a certain country, to parents of a certain origin. Those two factors will influence anyone's upbringing, the values one adopts, behaviors, attitudes, etc. Now for many people, the choice of a country to live in seems bound by the place one was born into. There is nothing wrong with it, also because most every country offers a choice of regions and cities with different particularities. Take France for example, a great country that has major metropolitan cities such as Paris, mid-sized cities like Bordeaux or Lyon, and thousands of wonderful smaller cities or villages to choose from, with different climates altogether. France counts Europe's highest mountain its own, and some of the nicest coastal areas on the Med or the Atlantic. Fabulous, isn't it? Needless to say, the exact same applies to Italy, Spain, the US and many others.

Still, this book states that for many readers, the fact to be born in one place or country, does not necessarily mean that it is the best place to make one happy. I call this concept "living a la carte". It means we ultimately have a choice. Just because I was born in Germany does not necessarily mean that I love beer, football, Schweinebraten and like to live in Germany more than anywhere else.

You get my point. Many of you may have already had the chance to grow up in several countries. You learned about the benefits these other places offered to your home country, but also some of the drawbacks they may represent. Several of you may have studied or worked abroad. These are invaluable experiences that have taught you about the impact of new and different ways of living.

In the end, we all have a CHOICE. We can decide to move on, and back, permanently or temporarily. This book argues that the only thing we don't have is the right to complain, to play victim. Ultimately, there are very few fixed cost and fixed elements in anyone's life. Ultimately, most everything is variable and can be changed. It's a bit overwhelming, but the concept embedded here is individual responsibility and choice. As simple as that.

Don't worry if you feel a bit of discomfort right now, or dizzy from the sensation that a lot has been thrown up in the air. In due course, the book will help you put it all together in a rather structured way.

For now, all that matters is that you understand, and hopefully agree, that your physical environment has an impact on your daily happiness. As such, it will be a key dimension to investigate as you progress on your road to more contentment.

2   Professional Impact on Society

The second, critical influencer to your level of satisfaction or the lack of it, is linked to your ability to have an impact on those around us. The argument is that we are all creatures that require a purpose to be fulfilled. We want to matter in other peoples' lives, not only in our relationship as a family member, a friend, spouse, but also in a professional manner.

Usually we call it work, and we lump it together with a means to make ends meet, to earn one's living. That would be, however, too much of a simplification for the purpose of this book.

For the goal of creating a path to a more fulfilled life, it is worth separating the financial aspects of work from the role it serves in our lives. The reason for this is obvious, in that one can choose a profession purely on its merits to provide a decent and predictable stream of income, but risk that it makes one unhappy every single day of our life.

You may think that this is pure theory. Not really! Studies have and continue to show that many people in organizations are not fully, or not at all, engaged in what they do. "Zombie employees" was a phrase created to capture this phenomenon. I would argue that many of us have accepted that neither we ourselves, nor those around us, are particularly happy because of what we do each day to pay our bills. Given that most full-time jobs are 8 hours-plus a day, 40 or more hours per week and that we tend to work 40 years plus, it is worth trying to improve from wherever you may be right now on the contentment curve.

Now you may say that it's a bit late for that if you are not at university or about to start your career. Well clearly, the earlier in your professional life you reflect on what you are doing, what aspects bring you joy vs. detract from it, and then act to move into directions where more of the elements of joy are present, the better you will be. No doubt about that. Still, I would say that it is never too late to start, because you will want to likely have a professional impact on society as long as you live.

Yes, you heard me well. I would firmly argue that even when your official professional career or job life is over, you will still want to find a way where you can add value to others beyond having a private relationship as described above. It's a different question whether you need and want to get paid for your contributions, and how much. The sheer fact of "being needed by others" and having a positive impact on them is what matters.

Some disclaimers upfront though. I would never want to say that all professional relationships are always perfect. There will always be elements that we perceive as tedious, but part of the package. Otherwise we'd likely call it a hobby, and then it would fit into the driver we will call "self fulfillment"– an activity we do merely for ourselves .

I would argue, however, that within any chosen field, there are plenty of choices, way more than I would be able to even imagine.

Back then when I was in business school, I was obliged to do summer internships each year. I used these as opportunities in several ways. First, to check different fields of work. In my case I was curious to experience the world of consulting compared to fast moving consumer goods companies (like Procter & Gamble, Nestle for instance), and banking. Second, I wanted to experience different cultures so I tried to do these internships in places I had not been to – let's park that dimension here for now.

By doing the internships in different companies of the same broader sector I experienced first hand how different the realities in each place felt. Whilst one company felt hierarchical, authoritarian, full of people with prestige and egos linked to their roles, the other was open, team-oriented and fact-based. As long as one had the facts straight and the better idea, one could succeed. Quite shocking how one corporate culture could be so different from the other. Can you imagine I had gone only to the organization I did NOT like and concluded, falsely, that fast moving consumer goods were not my thing...

My point is that whatever profession you have right now, there are plenty of dimensions you can change to improve your happiness. Let me suggest a few:

Size of the organization

The size of a company or institution will usually come along with different ways of working. If you are in a start-up team, chances are everyone has to do a bit of everything. If, however, you happen to work in a global company like for Nestle, with 300,000 employees, labour division and processes will be established, limiting the need (or ability) to work beyond you job description.

Private, Public or non-profit organization

Again, the incentives used to motivate people in either one of the types of organizations will vary largely depend on whether you find one single shareholder at the helm of a family or private equity set up, compared to a publicly quoted company with a sophisticated governance structure or even a non-profit organization. One can do the very same role and be very happy vs. unhappy in each of these environments.

Culture

This is probably the biggest driver and influence for anyone's willingness to fully engage, hold back or even leave an institution. It's the way things get done in your workplace that will see you either fit seamless or less so. That's always different from what's written on a paper in the corporate brochure or put on walls for others to quote them. Look at my previous example from two entirely different cultures that I experienced as an intern, from two very successful companies to this date in their respective fields. Both employ tens of thousands of people, hopefully most of them choosing one culture that suits them better over the other.

Micro factors

There is a myriad of micro factors starting with who you work for as your immediate stakeholder/boss. Someone once said that one always joins a company but leaves a boss. There is certainly more than an ounce of truth in it. Especially when you are young, you risk reporting into a boss who is not necessarily much older and experienced. So from a pure probability point of view, chances are you work for someone with average skills. After all, only a fraction of highly talented people will turn to outstanding leaders in their fields. So every now and then, just moving from one team to another can lead to enormous difference in personal engagement and success.

Other factors include

- Team members

Clearly who you spend a lot of time with will have an impact on your ability to succeed and to feel valued.

- Work load

The sheer amount of work usually correlates with one's happiness. Too much of a good thing and we tend to feel overwhelmed, our ability to deliver quality may suffer. Too little of workload, and we can get bored and look for something more challenging. It's a bit of an art to keep ourselves comfortably challenged.

- Project scope and duration (long vs. short term)

Some people prefer tasks that have a close to immediate impact. It is satisfying to see your accomplishments at the end of a working day. Not all jobs are geared up for that. In many fields it can take years, in some even decades, before the fruit of your labor are seeing the light of a customer or market. Not everyone can cope with that.

- Reach of scope of work

Certain jobs are highly personalized. If done well, you will change the life of an individual forever. Coaches, teachers, personal trainers for instance are in this field. Other jobs can have an impact on millions of people, but each impact may be much smaller. Imagine the organization or individual that invented and then commercialized the Velcro strip. Small but mighty impact for billions of consumers.

- Work-life balance

It's a bit related to the project load. Several jobs can be either done from home, a local office, or from being on the road for weeks without seeing home. Those difference will have an impact depending on how important it is for you to return or to be home everyday. Some love to travel for business and see the world that way. Others prefer to remain local.

- People vs Things focus

Every role, no matter where ist is, will have people as stakeholders to some degree, – be it as customers, suppliers, team members etc. It will be interesting for you to listen carefully into your self to find out if those relationships are more the lifeblood of your stimulation, or the drag that you have to deal with whilst you get things done. Conversely, most roles deliver some sort of "thing". Be it a product, service, craft or intellectual product. It's the task at hand. Very often, it's what gets us into a field of work in the first place. Again, it will be interesting to see if these items are still the source of your energy, or if they are now less relevant or even a key subtractor to your happiness.

As I sit here writing these lines, I cannot help but reflect on myself and my journey. For example, I miss those days where I had the luxury to concentrate on an in-depth market analysis for days on end. It was my job as an assistant brand manager to write the so-called Nielsen analysis each month. Years later, no role was neither requiring nor allowing me to ever spend that much time on an individual task.

And now, I realize how much I enjoy the prospect of hopefully adding value to you and your life, by spending a lot of my time dedicated to just one task – to write this short book that helps as many people as possible to get achieve a happier, more content life. What a luxury!

I hope I highlighted a few dimensions here that can have a profound impact on your individual happiness depending on your personal fabric, almost independent from the actual profession you have chosen or practice.

The point I am trying to make is that this book is not suggesting that the only way to get to a more fulfilled professional contribution to society (called job) is by changing one's occupation entirely. The suggestion I am putting out there is that there can be a momentous difference in satisfaction by gradually changing several components, like company culture, boss, team, project scope and load etc. So before you conclude that you "hate your job", wait and come along on the book's journey. You may learn that there are certain ASPECTS of your current way of PRACTICING your role that need changing to give you more satisfaction. The degree of difficulty and some of the consequences between choosing a radical job change vs. a gradual evolution based on your individual insights may prove insurmountable. Modifying he elements that can be easily changed and having an impact on your happiness clearly sounds like a better choice than the alternative of feeling like a victim without a option.

All these dimensions will hence play a role in your upcoming journey of self discovery further down in the book.

3   Relationships

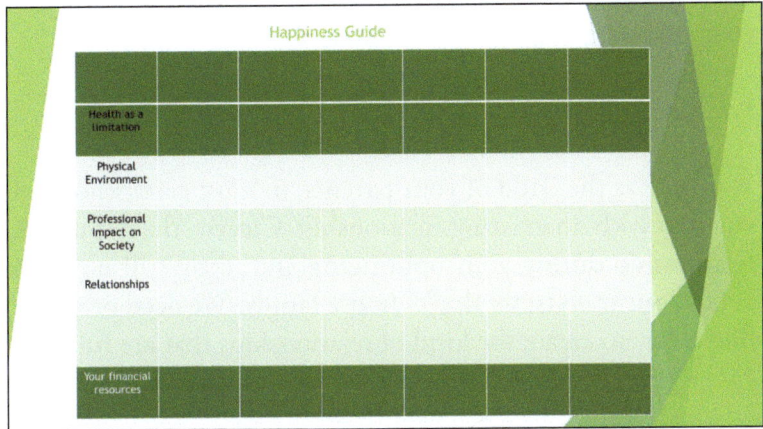

There is probably more written on the importance of relationships, and the degree to which they have a positive impact on us as human beings, than on any of the other drivers in this book. I will therefore not try to repeat much of it nor aim to give a significant addition to the body of work that's out there.

Let me though use this chapter to ensure that the dimensions of relationships are clear, so that when we go into operationalization of the drivers, you know what to look out for.

Relationships come in various forms in our lives. Individually, and in totality, they will have a strong impact on your ongoing happiness, life satisfaction, both on the positive, but unfortunately also on the negative side.

When you will go into listening mode to find out more about what makes you happy vs. unhappy in your daily life, as we will discuss shortly, you should pay attention to the following roles, as far as they apply or can potentially apply. The latter means that you may currently choose not to engage in certain roles whilst you could. That should also then be subject to your listening.

- Child

Your role as the child of your parents, in most cases known to you and with an existing relationship. Clearly, that's a critical relationship during your upbringing and likely still now. We choose our friends; we don't choose family. We need or should find a way to create the kind of relationships that are fulfilling vs. a drag. This should be a critical part of your journey.

- Sibling

Needless to say this may apply or not. If it does, it's a distinctly different relationship to other members of the family.

- Family at large

This may or may not play today an important part of your life. Chances are though that the degree of interaction will vary, depending on the life stage you are in, and the rest of your family.

- Friends

Probably a significant part of how you spend your life is not alone, but with friends. You should pay attention not only to each relationship individually, but also to whether you enjoy making new friends vs dread it or enjoy maintaining old friendships or not. Also, you may enjoy friends in groups more than individually, or vice versa.

- Significant other / Spouse / Relationship partner

Without going into all possible shapes and forms of relationships we can have with a lifelong partner, it's clear that the presence and absence of a trusted and loved partner, can either cause both tremendous happiness and fulfillment, or the opposite. It is rarely all good or all bad. It's about certain areas that are critical to enjoy, nurture and preserve, and others that may require a way to cope in tolerance, or change, or accept differences and related freedoms. It's again down to understanding better what "makes YOU tick" in the first place.

- Others

You may have coaches, mentors, teachers, spiritual leaders or others that play a significant role in your life. It will be critical to understand why you value them, to what extent you want to preserve and nurture them and what elements are distractors, risks to your relationship, and you therefore want to address them in some shape of form.

More so than with any of the other drivers, your intellectual honesty will be challenged when assessing the state of affairs in your relations. Just remember, it is not about assigning faults or credits, it is about getting to know your inner happiness fabric that matters. So, if certain aspects of any of the above relationships are not yet where they should be to help you lead a life of happiness and connectedness, then its best to face it now, in the intimacy of your own notes. Chances are that only then will you have a chance to improve. We will get back to operationalization in a short while.

For now, let's talk about the final dimension that we need to consider in analyzing your personal path to happiness.

4   Self Fulfillment

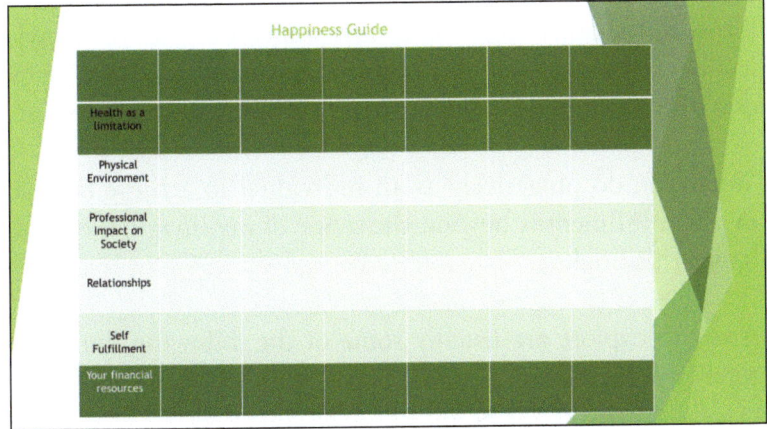

Now let us talk about the final dimension in my model to better understand what drives individual happiness.

Importantly though, if you strongly feel that there's a dimension missing, please don't hesitate to add it to the model. The model is flexible in that it can include as many distinct dimensions as you think there should be.

I for one, found that most other concepts can be classified without major trade off in the dimensions of this book. But who am I to judge your emotional fabric!

Now, let's talk about self-fulfillment.

Different from the impact you will want to have on society as a source of happiness, self fulfillment is all about YOU. It is about the things you do that provide you with a deeper sense of contentment, reflection, maybe mediation to get grounded, to renew yourself and feel balanced.

The argument of the book is that you may have a very fulfilled life in all the other dimensions such as relationships, your physical environment and your contribution to society, but if you don't invest sufficient time into self fulfillment, you miss out.

What you do proactively as an individual to achieve he goal of self-fulfillment is beyond the scope of my imagination and hence this book.

Areas to explore are usually some of the following, but definitely not limited to:

• The arts

No doubt that for many, the arts are a source of inspiration and reflection. Whether it is to practice them or to consume them as an observer – both are perfectly valid. Reflecting and reacting to art provides deep emotional feelings.

• Music

What would life be without music? Immersing yourself into a piece of music, listening to it with all your attention, can be a great source for self-fulfillment. Imagine listening to some of the greatest classically trained voices live in a concert hall with many other equally interested people. The moments of sheer perfection to experience are priceless for many. Now, you can replace classical music with any other form: jazz, rock and so forth. A friend of mine has been to 20 concerts of The Rolling Stones over the decades. He gets an immense sense of pleasure to listening to them and their music. Needless to say, playing an instrument, solo or in a group, can be equally (or even more) satisfying.

• Sports

Sports can be a source for many areas of this framework. You may decide to practice a certain sport to remain healthy, or to increase your chance of living a longer, happier life. That is one important side of sports.

The other is for making and maintaining relationships. Playing a round of team sports can be fun and a great platform to bond with friends, beyond the benefit of health it provides.

Then there is sport as a source of self-fulfillment. Running a marathon may be one of the most classical achievements many aim for in this area. Beating a certain time can be a subtlety of it. I would argue though that climbing mountains, crossing oceans, hiking certain trails like the Camino de Santiago, are all expressions of self-fulfillment, and not health-related sports activities.

It helps that our body produces all kinds of chemicals that enhance our sense of fulfillment during and after we practice sports.

- Nature / Exploration

I mentioned already that for me, being up close with nature is a wonderful source of self-fulfillment. The peace, quite and sensorial impressions are simply wonderful, including the change of the seasons.

You may want to try out a simple walk for 30 minutes to start. Then you can go further, with a 3 or 4 day hike through a beautiful national park and eventually a 3 week trek through the Himalayas – something I did 20 years ago and will never forget.

Or try to climb a mountain, or a hill. It's not coincidental that millions of people from almost all countries find a deep sense of fulfillment in climbing mountains. Turning around every now and then to see the changed point of view, to finally summit and feel a sense of accomplishment (combined with exhaustion), can be truly exhilarating.

I still remember having climbed Kilimanjaro in Africa with my wife 20 years ago. It was probably one of the single most important experiences to see the sun rise over Mawenzi peak in from the summit at almost 6000 m altitude.

- Spiritual

For many, this is an important dimension of existence, providing a deep sense of meaning and belonging to them. Taking the time to practice your religion of choice, or birth, is likely the most common way to access spirituality. Just taking a moment to pray, to converse with God, is likely to help you feel grounded, at peace and more self centered.

- Study

Life long learning is likely something you should consider and embrace as a source of self-fulfillment. Clearly, the world around us is changing rapidly and the body of knowledge is growing and changing with an ever-increasing pace. Learning should hence not be limited to a certain finite period of time. The sheer activity of learning something new may surprise you to be a great source of self-fulfillment. Ever fancied a degree in art, architecture? Maybe now is the time to start it...

- Travel

Somebody once said to me that "The world is a book and those who do not travel read only one page ". Personally, I can completely associate with it. To see different countries, cultures and languages as expressions of life, is almost a necessity for me. You may think that I exaggerate. Well, when Covid hit and most of us were no longer able to leave not only our houses, but also our countries, I quickly realized that whilst living in a beautiful place like Switzerland was indeed a privilege, it still could not replace the sensation linked to travel, to see something DIFFERENT. You may find that the need and pleasure linked to travel is hence similar to many other human needs, like hunger is to eating which then takes the need to eat away temporarily. Travel is similar.

- Various other hobbies

There is a myriad of other activities you may enjoy for your own benefit, such as cooking, writing, crafts, gardening. The opportunity is to overcome your complacency and to try them out at least once!

Funnily, Covid was seemingly an inflection point for many. Deprived of our ability to leave the house, many took up entirely new hobbies and fell in love with them.

So whether by practicing certain hobbies, or observing and consuming a sport or art, certain activities can be a regenerating force for good.

One challenge may lie in the fact that you don't know which area is your ideal source of self-fulfillment, simply because you did not have the time or energy to discover the one that suits you best. That's not a problem, but an opportunity.

Start with what you have already, even if it seems small. A walk in the forest or park, for example. The mere fact that you have found an activity you can practice pretty much all year round, at your will, and that it delivers the sort of emotions you need to be happy, is critical

From here, you can then explore other things to see if they compliment each other.

As I mentioned, I discovered that for me, nature plays a big part in self-fulfillment. Whether that is in hikes, bike rides, skiing, playing a round of golf or going for a swim in a lake. The sensation of being close to or one with nature has been very important.

During Covid though, alpine skiing was not possible. All ski stations were forced to close down for obvious reasons. I hence decided to try back-country (skinning) and cross-county skiing as replacement "therapies" ... and struck gold. Different to alpine skiing, with all its infrastructure, lifts and crowds, backcountry skiing helped me see nature up close and intimate. Now that the ski stations have opened up again, I only partially returned to alpine or downhill skiing, and have continued climbing up the hills on back country skis for sheer pleasure.

I am almost certain that by now you a) fully understand the concept of self-fulfillment and, b) have already a few ideas in mind on what you love to spend time on to get a sense of self-actualization and fulfillment. By the way, writing this book delivers a lot for me on this need.

As you will go into the next phase of self-discovery, stay alert and open to the moments and activities you enjoy for self-fulfillment. They may be as simple as for instance enjoying to rest in the afternoon sun on a bench in a park. Well, if that is so, then it's good to know about it, and plan for regular breaks, isn't it?

5 Self reflection and Assessment

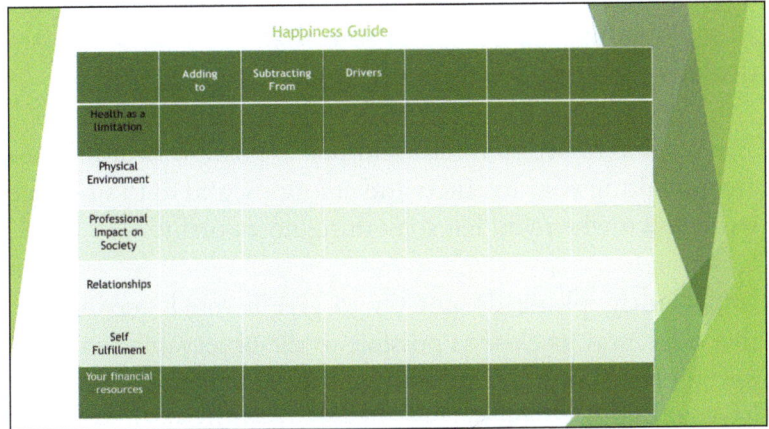

Now that you have a complete overview of the framework for your personal drivers of happiness, it is time to get into what's most important – to start paying attention to your emotional reactions over the next weeks and months.

Remember my example from the beginning of the book – I thought I knew that my issues were job related, when in fact I found out that I was simply affected every year at the same time by the grey of the Autumn weather. In hindsight, you may say that that's easy or obvious. Then I congratulate you and you may not need to read on, if you are already totally aware of everything that either adds or subtracts from your personal happiness level. For everyone else, I invite you to read on.

Now, what I want you to do over the next say 8-12 weeks is to carry a pack of post-its with you, and a pen. For those of you who are more technology savvy, please use notes or reminders in your phone instead.

What you will do is to jot down, at any given moment, anything that fills you with a sensation of happiness and joy, what it is that made you happy in this very moment. You will also write down when anything in your daily life makes you particularly unhappy, frustrated, or angry.

The key is a) to live your life as normal as possible to ensure you are not faking your instincts and emotions, and b) to stop, and write down when you felt something noteworthy.

Importantly, please do not try to give it much meaning at this stage, stay as close as possible to the observable facts. The interpretation of it all will be a second, distinct step, once you have collected a good deal of data about yourself.

Let me give you some examples for what good looks like, in random order, and not suggesting that these may apply to you:

Did not like:

- Having to take a shower in a cold bathroom
- Noise of the garbage truck outside
- Traffic jam on way to work
- Grey and cold weather
- Distance to job too long
- Don't feel listened to by my boss
- Lack energy to do sport.
- Feel exhausted from work. Need a break.

Liked a lot

- This afternoon conversation with my friend
- The new connection I made just now at the party

- The sun shining this afternoon on my way home
- New restaurant with great French food that I have just been to.
- Running this morning after work. Felt so relaxing.

What I want you to do is to jot these impressions down, unfiltered and unsorted for a number of weeks. The intent is to cover as many situations as possible of your real, daily life, so that the data you have on hand is a fair reflection of the underlying fabric of your satisfaction and dissatisfaction drivers.

It may feel a bit odd in the beginning. Think of it as trying a new sport or a new hobby. In the beginning any of that will feel clumsy but trust me, you will quickly get better at it. It will soon feel like second nature.

In fact, in the future, you will do these little moments of conscious recognition of moments of happiness and dissatisfaction automatically and instead of taking notes on a piece of paper, you will take notes mentally. That's when you have internalized the method and it becomes your self renewing process of progressing further in your happiness journey.

Once you feel like you have covered sufficient ground of your daily life, and you may run out of steam in finding new, additional moments of happiness or of frustration, you can move on to the next step.

Now, it is time to sort your notes. The intent is to identify patterns that are summarizing your individual notes on a slightly higher level. Call it the next level up, of meta level.

By grouping many notes together, I found out what mattered to me in the area of physical environment:

- Importance of green spaces close by my house – to walk, run and find peace after hours of work and city life.
- Importance of not more than 30 min commuting to work. Anything else would stress me. Anything much shorter would not let me unwind.
- Importance of a choice of good Mediterranean style restaurants in walking distance from home.

With just these few examples, I was able to essentially sit down over a map of the city I lived in and find the ideal area for me. By just moving a couple of hundred meters closer to a park and residential area with restaurants, I made a big change in my daily happiness.

Let me give you some more examples from the professional dimension of how to add value to society.

From all the notes, I realized the following underlying drivers of my happiness:

- To work on product categories that touch the lives of many people, not just a few. Clearly, I felt more at home in categories of mass consumption vs. say selling luxury goods to a happy few.
- To work across borders and cultures. I sensed that what I loved was to work on projects that had international reach, that required adaptation to cultural differences to work and be successful.
- To work in a culture where data and insights trumped opinions. I loved the fact that I worked in a company that

encouraged bottom-up leadership vs. leadership from pure experience or power.

I hope that some of these examples are helping to clarify what you are looking forward to uncover about yourself.

Ideally, you feel energized to start your journey. If you have already gone through the fact-finding phase, I hope that you feel a new energy as you review your happiness drivers. It can be very invigorating to make such great inroads into your innermost fabric.

No judgement is needed or helpful, especially when you get to the subject of your current relationships with friends, family members or your loved ones. Neither does cheating yourself really work nor help. It can be tough to face up to the issues you may have felt but suppressed in any of your relationships until now. Maybe this will help you bring them out in the open to be addressed, or at least you can then decide if it's worth keeping those relationships or not.

At the end of this stage, you should have at least 5-7 drivers in each area of satisfaction that represent you well.

6   Planning ahead

1   Y1 Plan

Happiness Guide						
	Adding to	Subtracting From	Drivers	Y1 Plan		
Health as a limitation						
Physical Environment						
Professional Impact on Society						
Relationships						
Self Fulfillment						
Your financial resources						

By now you will have a very good overview of what is ultimately required to make you happier in your daily life. The next step is to create a plan that programs a path forward to achieve more moments of happiness, and fewer of frustration. The basic underlying assumption is that if you can define milestones that reflect over time better on your identified drivers, the probability of you having good days goes up, and the likelihood of several, severe bad days goes down.

It's very simple if we take the example I gave in the previous chapter around the physical environment. For me, it was time to move into a quieter, slightly more upmarket, residential area away from major traffic, closer to a park and a nice set of restaurants. I hence set myself the 12 months / Y1 target of having accomplished such a move by then.

Similarly, based on what I learned regarding the drivers of my professional happiness, I set myself the target to work in a European role (vs. at the time a German market only role) with the next upcoming rotation.

I also decided to run at least 3x per week, to aim to climb a trekking peak in Nepal for self-fulfillment, to learn scuba diving and to start riding a motorbike again to work and on the weekends.

All these are examples of what I set myself as close-in targets 25 years ago. The benefit of making it a 12 months out target is that it's tough to delay things when you want to make them happen. As many of you know, the biggest issue when coming from any training is that in the first week back on the job, you go back to your normal routine, and then the training content is placed into the mental bookshelves of "could have, should have".

So go ahead, create your 12 months plan! What does success look like, even if its not a major step away from where you are today. Don't forget, it is not one single change that will make you happy, it's a bit of improvement in many areas of your life. So, no need to set yourself big, ambitious and probably unachievable tasks for year 1.

You may ask if we have not forgotten something important by now. Yes, we must also deal with our two limitations – money and health. Well, let's tackle the money side first. Plot down how much incremental it will cost you to put your plan into reality. How much does a move to a new place cost, how much the trip to Nepal, the motorbike and whatever else is coming with a sticker price. Doing the math will force you to prioritize and become creative. Instead of a new bike, you can buy a used one, or lease it in monthly installments. The trip to Nepal can cost a fortune if you did it in "style" or next to nothing if you did it explorer style with a trekking outfitter. It is the experience that matters, the finances can and have to flex to enable the journey.

I see this now play out on a totally different level. I love sailing and being on the water. There is something magical about sailing at night under a sky free from light pollution, waking up to dolphins swimming next to your bow. A friend of mine shares the same passion. We both dream of extended cruising and are determined to make it a reality. In fact, we have already executed our individual plans. I did it the "cheap" way, defining carefully how big and costly my boat must be to be able to do the trips I want to do, with the company that I need to host. I also did it smartly, chartering the boat out for the times that I won't need it, so that the income pays for all costs and even to pay for half the boat itself.

My friend decided to do it differently, starting with a much bigger boat, costing almost 3x mine. He then had to invite other partners / shareholders into the mix to pay for the boat. He actually decided to give up some freedom of usage to afford the bigger boat. He also had to hire a professional skipper, because the boat is too big and complex to be handled by himself. Again, a compromise I would have not liked very much.

The net is that you can share the same driver of "love sailing as a way to explore and be on the water" but your plan to get there may either be never feasible or within reach. It all depends on how you define it.

Allow me to say, though, that it would be surprising if the only way to get to the experience is one that is so costly that it's unattainable. The logic would then suggest that only a billionaire can truly be happy. I hope you agree with me that this is neither close to reality, nor a very sustainable idea. The world would be a worse place if everyone wanted to fly to Mars, have a super yacht so big that bridges have to be removed to allow it to navigate.... .

Try to get to 3-5 goals for the next 12 months, covering the totality of your 4 dimensions of happiness. It is best to aim for what is attainable vs. wishful thinking. There will be an opportunity to dream bigger later.

Finally, let's talk about health as the other limitation. Whether or not health will become a major limit to your plans for year 1 and beyond depends on two things – first, the kind of demands the drivers put on you and secondly, the kind of shape you are presently in.

If one of your planned elements includes an activity that is rather physically demanding, you will likely need to improve the shape you are currently in, , especially if you have led a sedentary lifestyle! On the other hand, you can assume that many things that are heavily linked to your health will not require any or only minor changes to your health regimen.

This is, however, a good moment to reflect and be honest with yourself. If weight has been an issue to your personal sense of happiness, then now is a good moment to tackle it. You can plan out a combination of actions that in combination have a high chance to improve your state of well being vs. today and deliver an improved feeling of contentment with yourself.

I had to realize that in order to climb the kind of mountains I had set my sights on, I had to step up my fitness regime rather significantly. Still today though, 30 years after I first put this system in place, I still do my 4k runs every second day, just to stay in reasonable shape to enjoy the many activities that enlighten my life.

2   End State

	Adding to	Subtracting From	Drivers	Y1 Plan		End State
Health as a limitation						
Physical Environment						
Professional Impact on Society						
Relationships						
Self Fulfillment						
Your financial resources						

Happiness Guide

Now that you have nailed your Year 1 plan, let's extrapolate a bit, and even dream a bit. What would be the end state of each of your drivers, if you dare to think it to the end, at least for now?

You notice that we jumped a column in the plan layout. That is deliberate and not a mistake. We come back to it in a short while.

So take a step back and ask yourself what would ultimately

represent the maximum or end-state of each driver to be close to certain that you would be fulfilled, happy and not have a sense of missing out in life.

You will end up with a picture of what your fulfilled, satisfied and happy life will look and feel like. No worries, you don't have to show it to anyone unless you choose to – which has benefits of its own in terms of inviting some of your loved ones into your dreams. It's fine to choose not to do so, and keep your plan close to your chest for now. This may help to have some more unconstrained thinking.

Take your time painting this picture. Then let it sit for a couple of days and revisit it. Check with how you react emotionally to it. Does it bring a smile on your face and feel amazing? If not, go back and reflect a bit more. You should feel like this is a dream you have painted for yourself, and that you would be very lucky and thankful if you were to get anywhere close to it, in totality. It is likely include several important, fulfilled friendships, one with a spouse, maybe children, the chance to give back to society, several plans to achieve self-fulfillment and to live in an environment that very much suits your needs and wants.

Can you also define the price tag that is most likely associated with this end state? How much would it take to save and invest over how many years to be able to put this dream into reality? Well, there is no better moment than right here and now to put things into motion and program the end-state. Remember, time is your friend if you start early enough!

Don't stop here, even if sticker price of your dream shocks you. Really plan out the financials. Start with how much you think your earnings are likely to grow, given your choices in terms of profession. Then decide how much you can put aside here and now, to enjoy the end state later. What's your expected return rate on these investments, how many years will it hence take to able to get there?

Well, now you have a rough idea and more importantly – you know what is enough to get you to your very own, personal dream. It's not necessarily the same as anyone else's. So comparing your dream with others is of limited use. You should sense a certain freedom from that. There is really no point in being or feeling like you are in the same rat race as everyone else.

First, hardly anyone has ever had the privilege to find out, like you just did, about what makes you happy, and what does not. Most other people are stuck in the circle of chasing more for the sake of hoping that an indiscriminate more is linked to more happiness. And even if they knew exactly what was required to make them happy, it would be different to your end-state and dream. So, there is really no point in comparing or even competing. Isn't that wonderful!?

Lastly, it may help to turn the end state of the individual drivers into a wholistic description, a painting of the end-state done in words. You may find it easier to write it as a letter to yourself, dated, telling yourself that one day, this is what you would like to look back on and how you will have wanted to live. I strongly believe in the prescriptive, or better yet, predictive power of putting your plans and thoughts onto paper. For some reason, it increases the likelihood of getting there tremendously.

3 In-between milestones

Happiness Guide						
	Adding to	Subtracting From	Drivers	Y1 Plan	In-Between Milestones	End State
Health as a limitation						
Physical Environment						
Professional Impact on Society						
Relationships						
Self Fulfillment						
Your financial resources						

In conclusion, you have now clarity about your underlying drivers of happiness, you have your distinct year 1 milestones identified, and you know the end state of what is most likely linked to your personal happiness – you know what is ultimately enough on all dimensions. You also know roughly how long it will take to get there, and what financial and health-related means it will require.

You have come a tremendously important way, in a relatively short period of time!

Now, in this last chapter, it is really up to you to define those in-between milestones that make the bridge between the fist year and the end-state. This could be a 5-year out snapshot, or it could be linked to a certain age of yourself. For instance, by the time that you turn 30 or 40. Your choice. Having at least one of these interim milestones should make your dream – more achievable goals on the one hand and also provide more teeth on the other – to deliver it and not risk running in place for too long.

Once you have decided and described a realistic milestone on your drivers for the chosen point in your lifeline, please take a step back. You have now finished the plan of this book, aiming to give you much more clarity on who you are, what makes you happy, and provided yourself with a vision and a plan on how to get there. Don't hold yourself accountable to the exact month or year. My prognosis is that you will surprise yourself how you almost automatically cruise on the path of happiness towards your end-state. The mind is a powerful organ, and it will guide you subconsciously on the way.

I hope you enjoyed this book and more importantly, your journey uo to here. I would be delighted to hear back from you, and to support you on your individual journey. Please don't hesitate to reach out via my LinkedIn profile.

Best wishes to you in your journey of self-discovery, and of what is enough to make you happy in every aspect of your life. I wish you the courage to pursue it.

About the author

Jörg P. Biebernick grew up in Germany, in a little village and of parents of moderate background. From relatively early childhood, he was keen to see the world beyond his town and country, to see what else there was out there. He was lucky enough to get into an excellent university with a scholarship, as his parents would have not been able to afford this private education. He then pursued a career in business leadership that took him to Switzerland, the USA, Belgium, back to Germany, back to the US and finally back to Switzerland, where he resides now. He was the member of several management boards at large, quoted companies, including Kimberly Clark as President Latin and South America, Imperial Brands PLC as President Europe and Co-CEO.

He is married for 23 years o a wonderful Cuban-American wife, has 2 teenage children and is currently taking a break from full-time work, also to write this book.

He welcomes feedback on the book and is happy to consider individual or organizational coaching. Please find him and his contact possibilities on LinkedIn.